VAMPIRE DREAMS

Suzy McKee Charnas

BROADWAY PLAY PUBLISHING INC
224 E 62nd St, NY, NY 10065
www.broadwayplaypub.com
info@broadwayplaypub.com

VAMPIRE DREAMS
© 2001 by Suzy McKee Charnas

All rights reserved. This work is fully protected under the copyright laws of the United States of America. No part of this publication may be photocopied, reproduced, stored in a retrieval system, or transmitted, in any form or by any means, electronic, mechanical, recording, or otherwise, without the prior permission of the publisher. Additional copies of this play are available from the publisher.

Written permission is required for live performance of any sort. This includes readings, cuttings, scenes, and excerpts. For amateur and stock performances, please contact Broadway Play Publishing Inc. For all other rights please contact the author c/o B P P I.

Cover photo by Rocky Heck

I S B N: 978-0-88145-190-0

First printing: June 2001
This printing: September 2016

Book design: Marie Donovan
Page make-up: Adobe Indesign
Copy editing: Sue Gilad
Typeface: Palatino

VAMPIRE DREAMS was originally produced by the Magic Theater (John Lion, Artistic Director; Harvey Seifter, Managing Director) in San Francisco as part of Springfest, opening on 21 March 1990. The cast and creative contributors were:

DOCTOR FLORIA LANDAUER........... Sandy Kelly Hoffman
DOCTOR EDWARD LEWIS WEYLAND........... Earll Kingston
KENNY .... Adrian Elfenbaum
LUCILLE .... Sharon Harrington
Director .... Michael Edwards
Stage manager .... Richard J Bloom

VAMPIRE DREAMS was subsequently produced by Bindlestiff Productions in San Francisco, opening on 13 November 1997 with the following cast and creative contributors:

DOCTOR FLORIA LANDAUER............................ Penny Benda
DOCTOR EDWARD LEWIS WEYLAND.............. Nick Scoggin
KENNY .... J J White
LUCILLE .... Esther Feuerstein

Voiceover..Jim Acker

Director & set design.. Rocky Heck
Set construction & house management .... Boho Hobos
Lighting design & operation.. Victor R
Slide operator & special effects .... Dan Weil
Original music.. Chrystene R Ells
Sound effects & engineering...................................... J J White
Sound operator, production and publicity coordinator ....Jill Heck

VAMPIRE DREAMS was produced in New York by Mefisto Theater Company, opening on 1 December 1999 with the following cast and creative contributors:

DOCTOR FLORIA LANDAUER.................... Carrie Wilshusen
DOCTOR EDWARD LEWIS WEYLAND............ Mark Nichols
KENNY .... Damien Midkiff
LUCILLE .... Kate Lunsford

Director .... Matthew von Waaden
Sets .... Jerome Martin
Costumes .... Alexandra Bredenko
Lighting .... Matt Dacey
Composer/sound designer .... Will Pitts

CHARACTERS & SETTING

DOCTOR FLORIA LANDAUER, *therapist, a mature woman*

DOCTOR EDWARD LEWIS WEYLAND, *a new client, a middle-aged, attractive academic type. Slightly accented English is not inappropriate for this character.*

KENNY, *a client of* FLORIA*'s, a young man*

LUCILLE, *a colleague of* FLORIA*'s*

The action takes place in New York City, in the present.

ACT ONE

(The office of DOCTOR FLORIA LANDAUER *in Manhattan. A swivelchair, desk, phone, answering machine, tape recorder. A window, bookshelves, assorted bric-a-brac.)*

FLORIA: You've left a line blank on our intake form. Isn't there anyone I can contact in case of an emergency?

WEYLAND: No.

FLORIA: No one close to you?

WEYLAND: This is my choice of "life style."

FLORIA: You do understand that therapy is a close encounter?

WEYLAND: Yes. We don't always get what we want, Doctor.

FLORIA: What do you want, Edward?

WEYLAND: To return to my work.

FLORIA: So you like teaching at Cayslin?

WEYLAND: It's the usual academic environment—an ivory jungle. It suits me.

FLORIA: Sounds dangerous.

WEYLAND: Oh, yes. No one goes for the jugular like an irate academic.

FLORIA: Dean Sharpe is a soft-hearted specimen, then. He's concerned about you.

WEYLAND: He forced me to come here. That is not my idea of concern.

FLORIA: He referred you to me. Whether we work together or not is your choice.

WEYLAND: If the choice were mine I wouldn't be here.

FLORIA: It must have been a tough call, putting an eminent professor on unscheduled, open-ended leave. But that's his problem. What's yours?

WEYLAND: *(Pause)* I seem to suffer from the delusion that I am a vampire.

FLORIA: A vampire.

WEYLAND: Yes.

FLORIA: Someone who drinks other people's blood.

WEYLAND: Is there another definition?

FLORIA: And you've had this idea about yourself for how long?

WEYLAND: A year or so.

FLORIA: On what evidence?

WEYLAND: Don't toy with me, Doctor. I attacked a woman at Cayslin and tried to drink her blood. She resisted, I panicked and ran. Dean Sharpe must have told you. I count myself lucky that he hasn't told the media as well.

FLORIA: He said that you disappeared for more than two months. He didn't mention vampires.

WEYLAND: He doesn't know.

FLORIA: If he does, he's not telling.

WEYLAND: But you know, now.

FLORIA: I don't tell either. You do, I don't. That's the set-up here.

ACT ONE

WEYLAND: I assume that this will be my regular hour. *(He exits.)*

(Scene shift)

(FLORIA *alone*)

FLORIA: *(To tape recorder)* New client, Edward Lewis Weyland: personal history, ordinary—more than ordinary, positively bare. Only child of European immigrants, schooling normal, field work unexceptional, academic posts leading to tenure at Cayslin. Married never, kids none, no living family, no religion. Previous mental illness, none. No signs of alcohol or drug-related problems. Therapy is the condition of returning to his classroom. A good thing too, by the sound of things so far. *(To intercom on desk)* Hilda, any messages? Still nothing from my daughter? How can I make plans if she won't let me know when she's due into the city? What? Oh, damn—I thought we'd dropped Kenny. No, give me a minute, then send him in.

(Scene shift)

(FLORIA *and* KENNY *in session*)

KENNY: So what do you think, Doctor Landauer? I mean, does it sound like something I could handle?

FLORIA: How do you feel about it, Kenny?

KENNY: I told you, I'm scared. What if they reject me again?

FLORIA: Isn't the question really, what if they accept you?

KENNY: You're the shrink, you tell me.

FLORIA: Try speaking for me. Let's hear what kind of advice I would give you.

KENNY: That's such crap. One part of me talks like you, and then I have a dialog with myself: "Hi,

Doc, I'm your patient and I've got problems." "Hi, Kenny, your problem is, you're a dork. Take care of it yourself."cYou just sit there while I do all the work.

FLORIA: You've been coming here for two years. You know my therapeutic style by now.

KENNY: Yeah, and I don't like it. I want something from you.

FLORIA: *(Signal beeps)* Kenny, your hour is up.

KENNY: It's all just a lot of boring shit to you, isn't it? You don't care.

FLORIA: Next time, Kenny.

(KENNY *exits.*)

FLORIA: *(To tape machine)* Another miserable session. Details later, Hilda, it's too depressing. Off the record: how can I help when what I really want to do is drop-kick the little nerd into the middle of Central Park?

(LUCILLE *enters.*)

LUCILLE: Wasn't that Kenny stomping down the hall? I thought you referred him out.

FLORIA: I sent him to Mel Green last week, but Kenny showed up here today at his usual time. What do I have to do to get across to that kid, jump out the window?

LUCILLE: Use some muscle, kiddo. We're in charge here, remember?

FLORIA: I'm not. My Wednesday group was awful—like trying to push a polar bear through a mail slot. Was I ever good at this stuff?

LUCILLE: Brilliant, but self-doubt is part of the job. Maybe it's time to take that up again at the colloquium—how we handle our own reactions to difficult clients.

ACT ONE

FLORIA: Well, how do we? We work with them and work with them, and then they go make the same dumb, self-destructive choices all over again. It's like being trapped at the baggage carousel in the airport, watching the same damned black nylon bags going around and around and around all looking alike.

LUCILLE: Wow. Feeling a little burnt out, are we?

FLORIA: Crisped. Carbonized. Except—you'll never guess what walked in here today. What's up, I say. He says: "I seem to suffer from the delusion that I'm a vampire."

LUCILLE: You are kidding!

FLORIA: Nope, that's what he told me. Right off the bat, as it were.

LUCILLE: I am going to die of envy. Would you trade him for an agoraphobic dentist?

FLORIA: Not for a million bucks. Go find your own monster, Lucille.

(Scene shift)

(FLORIA *and* WEYLAND *in session*)

FLORIA: Edward, do you remember your dreams?

WEYLAND: I don't dream.

FLORIA: Will you close your eyes for me now, as if you were sleeping?

WEYLAND: Why?

FLORIA: Sometimes I'll ask you to do things that seem whimsical or strange. It's all part of the therapeutic process. Will you close your eyes now? Good. How do you feel?

WEYLAND: *(More tense than before)* Uneasy. What I don't see can hurt me.

FLORIA: Like what? What might hurt you?

WEYLAND: A vampire's enemies, I suppose. Peasants, with torches.

FLORIA: Edward, open your eyes and tell me what you see.

WEYLAND: I see a woman with a clever face. Her blouse—a "peasant"-style blouse I believe—has a food stain on the left side. You don't write as we speak, Doctor Landauer. Are you recording our conversations on tape?

FLORIA: No. I do make notes afterward, but they're kept strictly confidential.

WEYLAND: And what do your notes about me indicate thus far?

FLORIA: That we need to find out more about this "vampirism" and discover what has led you to adopt such a construct.

WEYLAND: And then you persuade me to give up my delusion and become what the world takes for normal.

FLORIA: Is that how you see our project here?

WEYLAND: Dean Sharpe needs a written testament to my mental stability before he can invite me back to Cayslin. That is my project.

FLORIA: What about exploration, understanding, the background work for healing?

WEYLAND: That sounds unpleasantly open-ended. How long does it take?

FLORIA: How do you experience your face at this moment?

WEYLAND: As being on the front of my head. Why?

FLORIA: Bear with me. I see so much tension in your face—will you let me help?

(FLORIA *reaches toward* WEYLAND. *He recoils.*)

ACT ONE

WEYLAND: I do not enjoy being made ridiculous.

FLORIA: I only meant to try to relax your face with massage.

WEYLAND: This is supposed to be a talking cure.

FLORIA: I'm sorry. I wanted to shift us off the intellectual plane but I was in too much of a hurry; like you, Edward. I know you're eager to regain your inner balance, but that's the goal, not the starting point. In between is the process.

WEYLAND: Process? It's a farce.

FLORIA: It's also your route back to Cayslin.

WEYLAND: Thank you for the reminder that I am not here by choice. Let me remind you that my time is valuable too. Will a month be long enough for you to do your job?

FLORIA: Depends. Do you want me to take your situation seriously, or not?

WEYLAND: My situation is ridiculous. My work waits while I stumble around in this kindergarten that you call your process.

FLORIA: Don't shout at me, Professor, this isn't your classroom. What are your hands doing?

WEYLAND: Is this another of your stupid games?

FLORIA: Yes. Your hands. What are they doing?

WEYLAND: Struggling.

FLORIA: Struggling with what?

WEYLAND: I don't know. You don't know either.

FLORIA: No, but between us we can find out.

WEYLAND: You think your tricks can uncover my secrets?

FLORIA: Yes, if I do my job well. I'm game to try. Are you?

WEYLAND: Suppose I say yes? What would you ask of me right now?

FLORIA: Talk to me about being a vampire. I don't mean, give a lecture. Contemplate aloud, describe. Use your imagination.

WEYLAND: I don't have to imagine what is real for me.

FLORIA: But I do. Help me, Edward.

WEYLAND: I hunt.

FLORIA: Where? How? What sort of—of victim?

WEYLAND: You can dismiss the obvious possibilities, for a start. Homeless people sleep outdoors, but their blood tends to be sour with drugs, disease, or liquor. It's the same with those who cruise the bars and clubs. I can detect illness by the odor of the skin. Why take chances? I choose my hunting grounds carefully—gallery openings, museums, department stores—places where women may be approached.

FLORIA: Only women?

WEYLAND: Very good, Doctor Landauer. Hunting women is time-consuming and expensive. I also frequent places where homosexual men seek others of their kind.

(Signal beeps.)

FLORIA: I'm sorry, Edward, our time—

WEYLAND: I'm not finished. Choosing a healthy victim, I present myself as a professional man, repressed, fastidious, not a disease carrier or a homophobic maniac. I invite him to my hotel. I drink his blood. Now, I think, our time is up.

(WEYLAND *exits as the beeper sounds.*)

ACT ONE

(Scene shift)

(FLORIA, alone, listens to Doug Sharpe's voice on her message machine)

VOICE: Floria, I need a reading on Weyland. People here want to start a search to replace him, which I don't want to do. So what's it all about? The favorite in-house theory is that he blew his celebrated cool and ran off with some irresistable undergraduate. Speaking of which, oh flower of my heart, how about running off with me to the ballet next week? All work and no play makes the therapist crazy.

(Scene shift)

(FLORIA and LUCILLE)

LUCILLE: You don't need the colloquium, you need a mindless week on a beach.

FLORIA: So who wants me off the program? Jacoby, right? He hates women who don't smile all the time.

LUCILLE: You're crabby as Hell this morning. What's going on?

FLORIA: My daughter is driving me crazy. She wants me to babysit the kids while she and Keith go sightseeing here during his conference next month. I love my grandchildren, but the baggage that comes with them—

LUCILLE: Baggage again. You really do need a vacation.

FLORIA: What's the point of having a daughter who's more conservative than your own mother was? I should have cats. Cats are supposed to be conservative.

LUCILLE: Come on, Sarah's a peach compared to most therapists' kids.

FLORIA: You don't have to listen to her abysmal politics. And she needles me about Doug Sharpe. She hates it that I'm not pushing to get married again. Who's the Mom here, anyway?

LUCILLE: Hey, at least she cares.

FLORIA: I have a feeling that her own marriage is in trouble. And you know what? I do not want to hear it. I'm so sorry for her, but I'm tired of being blamed for everything that I warned her against in the first place.

LUCILLE: Okay. What else?

FLORIA: What else, what?

LUCILLE: What else?

FLORIA: Alice Gibbs went back into a detox unit last night.

LUCILLE: Good, if that's where she needs to be. Don't be so hard on yourself, you're not God. Without your help Alice couldn't have handled the big, bad world as long as she has.

FLORIA: I don't know how you keep your head above water, Luce, I swear I don't. I used to know how, but I think I've lost it.

LUCILLE: How's your vampire? Hilda tells me he's cute, in a seasoned sort of way.

FLORIA: Cute isn't the word I'd use, exactly.

LUCILLE: Better than cute? Oh-oh, do I detect a yen for his venerable body?

FLORIA: I've got a mature academic, thanks. I don't collect them like Hummel figures.

LUCILLE: Seriously—

FLORIA: Seriously, this client is probably transmuting into the vampire role some aspect of himself that he finds unacceptable. In other words, he's gay, and that can be rough going for a man of his generation. But what an original way to resist!

ACT ONE

LUCILLE: Sounds like there might be a book there—a monograph at least.

FLORIA: The thought had crossed my mind.

LUCILLE: What better way to show Jacoby what an ass he is?

(Scene shift)

(FLORIA *alone*)

FLORIA: *(To tape recorder)* I don't know why I'm so restless, so out of synch with my clients. Not that that stops them; it doesn't even slow them down. They keep on nibbling away, nibbling away, sharp little teeth going snip, snip, snip. I'm not so light on my feet any more, I can't do the dance that lets you help but keeps you out of striking range. I used to have a sort of inner choreographer that hardly ever let me put a foot wrong. Lately, there's nothing. I keep wanting to yell at them, there must be more to you than this! There must be more to me.

(Scene shift)

(FLORIA *and* WEYLAND *in session*)

WEYLAND: Your décor is appalling. Where did you get all this?

FLORIA: Clients bring me things.

WEYLAND: Isn't it compulsive behavior, keeping all the rubbish people hand you? Perhaps you should see a psychiatrist.

FLORIA: Tell me about your office at Cayslin.

WEYLAND: My office at Cayslin is tasteful. Organized. Spare.

FLORIA: Like your life there.

WEYLAND: Like my life.

FLORIA: Yet you broke out of your spare, organized, academic life in a particularly colorful way. Edward, tell me what you keep on your desk.

WEYLAND: Suppose you're right? Suppose I broke out of my life as a man breaks out of prison. Is this the way to break back in?

FLORIA: Are you sure you want to?

WEYLAND: Why else would I keep coming back here? It's not safe. Some one has been following me, someone from this office.

FLORIA: Who? Peasants with torches?

WEYLAND: It's paranoid, surely, to see paranoia everywhere?

FLORIA: You were telling me last time about preying on homosexuals. When you pick up a man, is it a paid encounter?

WEYLAND: If those are the terms, yes.

FLORIA: How do you feel about having to pay?

WEYLAND: Why not? Others work to earn their bread. Why shouldn't I use my earnings to pay for my sustenance?

FLORIA: Once you're alone with your quarry, how do you—attack?

WEYLAND: Firm pressure on the neck, here, interrupts the flow of blood to the brain, causing unconsciousness. Getting close enough to apply that pressure isn't difficult.

FLORIA: You do this before or after any sexual activity?

WEYLAND: Before, if possible. And instead of.

FLORIA: And you generally hunt men in preference to women?

ACT ONE

WEYLAND: A practical necessity. Historically women have been locked away like prizes, or else so worn down by repeated childbearing as to be unhealthy prey for me. That's changing now, but men are still preferable. How carefully you control your expression, Doctor Landauer—no trace of disapproval. Yet you see me, I'm sure, as one who victimizes the already victimized. That is the world's way.

FLORIA: Like a wolf bringing down stragglers at the edge of the herd?

WEYLAND: Except that I can feed without killing. Often my victim is unaware of having been attacked.

FLORIA: Is it important to you not to kill?

WEYLAND: Why advertise my presence with a trail of drained corpses? We are talking about my life here, not a film entertainment for imbeciles.

FLORIA: Can you put yourself in the mind of a homosexual victim and describe an encounter from his point of view?

WEYLAND: No. Our time is up.

(He exits as signal beeps.)

(Scene shift)

(FLORIA alone)

FLORIA: *(Speaking to recorder)* How much of his "vampirism" does he act out, how often? This secret and powerful identity is so cleverly constructed that I forget to do the work that needs doing here. He must be very strong to have maintained his career under this intense interior pressure. If only I can find a way to free that strength. He makes me ambitious.

(Scene shift)

(FLORIA and WEYLAND in session)

FLORIA: We were talking about sex.

WEYLAND: We were talking about hunting.

FLORIA: Then it's time we talked about sex.

WEYLAND: Really. Do you enjoy wringing confessions of solitary vice from men of mature years?

FLORIA: Under what circumstances do you find yourself sexually aroused?

WEYLAND: Whenever I pass a post office. *(No response)* Most usually upon waking from sleep.

FLORIA: What do you do about it?

WEYLAND: The same as others do. I am not a cripple. I have hands.

FLORIA: Do you fantasize at these times?

WEYLAND: No.

FLORIA: You don't think about drinking blood?

WEYLAND: While similarly engaged, do you visualize chocolate mousse?

FLORIA: How do you feel, Edward, about your victims' sexual expectations of you?

WEYLAND: They don't interest me. Unlike your kind, I know the difference between predation and sex.

FLORIA: What about female vampires?

WEYLAND: I've never met one.

FLORIA: I thought people who die of vampire bites become vampires themselves.

WEYLAND: Too many movies, Doctor. I am not a communicable disease.

FLORIA: Then how does your kind reproduce?

ACT ONE

WEYLAND: I have no kind, and why should I reproduce? I may live for centuries, perhaps indefinitely. I would be foolish to father my own rivals.

FLORIA: Ah. Not much elbow-room up there at the top of the food chain.

WEYLAND: Precisely. My sexual equipment is clearly only biological mimicry.

FLORIA: But you do have the standard male organs?

WEYLAND: Do I detect a note of prurient interest, Doctor Landauer? Something akin to pausing at the cage to watch the tigers mate?

FLORIA: How would you feel about that?

WEYLAND: I feel very tired of turning and turning on the tiny axis of how I feel.

FLORIA: How small an axis is that, Edward? Can you walk the circumference of your feelings here in my office?

WEYLAND: One pirouette on point would suffice.

FLORIA: So you have no urge to sleep with anyone?

WEYLAND: Would you mate with your livestock? Your skepticism is blindingly apparent, Doctor Landauer. Let me be just as plain. Women, and men for that matter, appeal to me very little. My sex urge is of low frequency and easily dealt with unaided. I can perform if I must, but unlike humans I am not obsessed.

FLORIA: So you're not human at all. You aren't human, you've never been human—

WEYLAND: Make the jump, you can do it: and I never will be human.

FLORIA: Then you see yourself as—what? Some sort of mutation?

WEYLAND: Perhaps your kind is the mutation.

FLORIA: You don't like humans, do you, Edward?

WEYLAND: Humans are mere cattle, yet my entire life revolves around them. I entertain them with lectures about themselves, read their wretched papers and test their hot little minds. I endure their meetings and their parties and all their puerile, eager appetites, while keeping always alert to how dangerous they can be. I hide myself in the churning herds of men, and I hate them.

FLORIA: What do you feel now in your body?

WEYLAND: I feel tension.

FLORIA: What are you doing with your hands?

WEYLAND: I press my hands to my stomach.

FLORIA: Can you speak for your stomach?

WEYLAND: "Feed me or die."

FLORIA: Answer. Answer, Edward.

WEYLAND: "Will you never be satisfied?" No!—You will not seduce me into quarreling with the terms of my existence.

FLORIA: What terms, Edward? What are those terms?

WEYLAND: The gut determines. That first, everything else follows.

FLORIA: Say, "I resent—"

(WEYLAND *is silent.*)

FLORIA: "I resent the power of my gut over my actions."

WEYLAND: I resent your arrogant assumption that you have the slightest insight into my life.

FLORIA: Insight is our quarry in this office, Edward. We pursue it here together.

(WEYLAND *exits.*)

ACT ONE

(Scene shift)

FLORIA: *(To tape)* Well, I wanted relief from the Kennys of the world and here it is. He talked quite coolly today about a man he killed—

WEYLAND: *(From another part of the stage)* Inadvertently.

FLORIA: —by drinking too much from him.

WEYLAND: He was a student of mine.

FLORIA: A fantasy of bloody revenge for years of classroom frustration?

WEYLAND: It amuses me to cultivate the minds inhabiting the bodies that contain my food.

FLORIA: The delusion may be fed by work pressures. I suggested a change of jobs.

WEYLAND: Too risky. And I might have to take a position lower on the professional ladder.

FLORIA: Status seems important to him. Well, what self-respecting vampire has ever claimed to be less than minor nobility?

WEYLAND: An eccentric professor is one thing, an eccentric pipe-fitter another. And I like expensive cars.

FLORIA: Edward asserts that he has lived many human lifetimes, but forgets the details during periods of suspended animation in between. He has already chosen a hiding place for his next long sleep, a disused subway spur. He doesn't like to talk about this.

WEYLAND: It's not a pleasant subject. I only resort to this long sleep when I have no other choice. Each time I go to earth the odds against me lengthen.

FLORIA: So he's built a threat into the fantasy. Maybe that's why he offers no details about the hibernation process itself.

WEYLAND: The essence of this state is that I sleep through it—not an ideal condition for scientific observation.

FLORIA: I set him a hurdle and he just flies over it. His swings between fantasy and reality are absolutely breathtaking.

WEYLAND: I've been reading in your field, Doctor Landauer. You work from Gestalt theory, do you not?

FLORIA: Originally, yes.

WEYLAND: Then you think that I project some ugly aspect of myself onto others whom I then treat as my victims. An idea of mind-numbing banality, if I may say so. Well. Will you forgive me for having indulged my fantasy here in your office? I've only been storing up my poor, illusory pleasures against the inevitable moment when I must give up my imagined self.

FLORIA: Give it up for what, Edward?

WEYLAND: For banality, of course. The life of an aging academic is bounded by his study, his classroom, and his office—meetings, conferences, the summer jaunt abroad, the occasional creaking affair. An enchanting prospect.

FLORIA: We're not there yet. Your perspective may change.

WEYLAND: What do you mean, "We're not there yet?"

FLORIA: We still have work to do.

WEYLAND: But today I see right through my phantom self with his pathetic secrets. Carpe diem, Doctor; let's get rid of him while the window of opportunity is open.

FLORIA: We're not ready for that.

WEYLAND: I think we are.

ACT ONE

FLORIA: Look, you can walk out of here for good right now. But if I close your file today, my report to Dean Sharpe won't say what you want it to say.

WEYLAND: That's blackmail, Doctor.

FLORIA: Tell me about your colleagues at Cayslin.

(Scene shift)

FLORIA: *(Talking on phone)* Let me get a word in edgewise, will you, hon? Sare, it doesn't do any good—I know it's not fair. I know; but I can't tell you what to do, and if I did—sweetheart, for that kind of advice you go to a marriage counselor. I'm not ducking your problems, I'm just—Sarah? *(Hangs up)*

(LUCILLE *enters.*)

FLORIA: It's killing me, Luce: she's so unhappy, and somehow it's all my fault.

LUCILLE: All these years in the relationship business, and this surprises you?

FLORIA: But it's such a cliché! After buying the traditional program—early marriage, instant babies, part-time work so she could be with them—Sarah starts to realize that I wasn't actually certifiable when I suggested waiting, starting a career of her own, the whole boring feminist thing. She's just noticed that if that marriage goes she'll have hung herself out to dry, babies and all.

LUCILLE: And you're supposed to fix it, right? Well, you can't, and you shouldn't try.

FLORIA: I know that. She knows that. We're going through the motions anyway. It makes me feel like an idiot. The parent-and-child thing is just beyond me. I think I should have been sterile. I should have been a sterile orphan.

LUCILLE: You should have taken serious time off last year, after your mother died. You know what I said at the time—

FLORIA: Yes, I do, I was there when you said it.

LUCILLE: —grieving is major work, and it's harder if you don't face up to your own fear of death.

FLORIA: Lucille, I'm not talking about the fear of death—

LUCILLE: No, not then; and not now, I notice.

FLORIA: Come on, cut it out. I just wonder sometimes how it would feel to have no kids, no ancestral ghosts behind you, no inevitable, personal doomsday looming ahead.

LUCILLE: Nuts.

FLORIA: What?

LUCILLE: It would feel crazier than shit and lonesome as Hell, ask any psycho who thinks he's God almighty or Frankenstein's monster. Now that's settled, can we review some cases here?

(Scene shift)

(Night. WEYLAND, alone in FLORIA's office, listens to her tape machine.)

FLORIA: *(Voice on tape)* I used the word "monster" today, deliberately. He protested. "I think of myself as a prodigy of Nature," he said. He ages, he believes, very slowly during his waking periods, so he thinks his origins go back incredibly far, maybe into prehistory. He retains only some general knowledge from one lifetime to another, and he's proud of deducing the rules of his "vampire" existence from current evidence alone. For example, he thinks his body has a unique chemistry that extracts enough nutrients from human blood for him to live on. Neat trick.

ACT ONE

WEYLAND: You should know, Doctor. You have so many neat tricks of your own.

(Scene shift)

(FLORIA *and* WEYLAND *in session*)

FLORIA: Edward, can you speak for blood?

WEYLAND: Let me see. "I flow to the heart's soft drumbeat through lightless prisons of flesh. I am rich, I am nourishing, I am difficult to attain. Patient, steady, I work unnoticed, a hidden thread of vitality running from age to age, beautiful, complex, efficient..." That was almost as good as a meal.

FLORIA: Let's pursue this. You've talked about hunting before, but only in the abstract. Can you describe a particular hunt for me now, in detail?

WEYLAND: I am in your hands, Doctor. Let's say—a poetry reading at the 92nd Street Y. I scan the audience for candidates. A woman sits in front of me, alone. She wears a blouse with an invitingly low neckline. No perfume—good. Strong scents irritate me. At intermission I approach, I make a slighting comment about the reading. She agrees. We adjourn to a coffee shop on 86th Street. She believes my shy-academic act. My clothes, my manner, the eyeglasses I wear, all are chosen to reinforce it. She is a copy editor at a publishing house. I offer to escort her home. She settles beside me in the taxi, talking about books. I extend my arm along the back of the seat behind her. Traffic is heavy, the cab moves slowly. There is time to make my meal right here if I act quickly.

FLORIA: You'd take that risk?

WEYLAND: I get so tired of caution sometimes! And my hunger is powerful, not like your puny human appetite. My excitement is high. The words I speak, the way I look at her, every gesture is part of the hunt.

There is added excitement because I am stalking my quarry in the presence of a third party—the driver. I press the place on the woman's neck. She slumps against me. In the stale interior of the cab, to the murmur of the radio, I take hold at the tenderest part of her throat, here. I taste salt on her skin just before I strike. My saliva thins her blood. I draw her richness into my mouth, swiftly, before she can wake, before we can arrive. My mind floats, my body heats with energy.

FLORIA: And then?

WEYLAND: I shake her gently by the shoulders. She comes around, bewildered, weak, thinks she fainted. I instruct her doorman to see that she reaches her apartment safely. My victim, thinking perhaps that if not put off by her "illness" I would accompany her upstairs, gives me her telephone number. I walk back to my hotel, lifted on the surge of power that feeding brings. When this abates, I sleep.

FLORIA: How did you feel about your victim as a person?

WEYLAND: She was food.

(Scene shift)

*(*FLORIA *alone)*

FLORIA: *(On phone)* Douglas, you know I can't promise a successful outcome let alone supply a timetable. So tell them to hold their horses. His colleagues don't like him much, do they? He's "not easy"—I love professorial understatement. Oh, yes, he is attractive. Don't be jealous, sweetie, you know I'm only allowed to fix my clients, not fall for them. Yes, it's been too long. Good God, Douglas. The only people who talk dirty to me on the phone are academics. No, idiot, not him, you! Yes, that would be nice. Who's dancing? Okay, you're on.

ACT ONE

(Scene shift)

(FLORIA *and* WEYLAND *in session*)

WEYLAND: I saw you at Lincoln Center last night, with Dean Sharpe. I didn't know that you and he were a couple.

FLORIA: What were you doing at the ballet?

WEYLAND: The same as you: watching the dancers. I enjoyed it. I don't know why. Do you? Can you see something here that I don't see?

FLORIA: What do you see?

WEYLAND: Dance begins as a pantomime of the chase among hunter-gatherers everywhere. But when a man and a woman dance together as they did last night, it's different. One is hunter, one is prey, and they shift these roles between them. Yet I feel some other level of significance—sex, I suppose. I feel it... *(Touches his solar plexus)* ...as a tugging sensation, here. What is it, this pull so like hunger but not hunger?

FLORIA: Edward, can you speak for your hands?

WEYLAND: "We are similar. We seek the comfort of like closing with like."

FLORIA: If you were to find a likeness—a partner you could dance with—

WEYLAND: No. I've told you: I am a solitary being and content to be so.

FLORIA: In that case, Edward, we're finished here. I can't help you.

WEYLAND: You are too modest, Doctor—you already have, much against my initial expectations. So much honesty must be healthy, for a life as dependent on deception as mine.

FLORIA: You and I don't mean the same thing by "health".

WEYLAND: More than health is at stake. My methods of self-discovery are few. There is no one like myself that I can look at and learn from. Any tools that show me to myself are valuable to me—even the tools of your trade, Doctor.

FLORIA: Even those? But self-discovery is just a start. We all want to be seen as we are and honored for what we are by someone else who shares our perceptions. But if I see you—if I really see you—

WEYLAND: You do see me—you begin to see me. What will come of that, do you think?

(Scene shift)

(FLORIA *alone*)

FLORIA: *(To tape)* I hit a wall with him today and he drew me through it, deft as a surgeon. If there is a book here, someone else will have to write it. I try to write about him but the vocabulary is all wrong. There is no vocabulary. I don't know how to manage my feelings about him, let alone write them down. I'm ashamed to write them down. I dreamed of myself with him in a taxi, like the woman from the poetry reading—and what in God's name was that anyway, if not a delusion too strong for me to crack? The impact is all the other way, to judge by my dream: he was utterly focused, with the absorption a woman wants from a man in bed. No scorekeeping, no fantasies, just the senses, the moment, appetite overriding all.

(WEYLAND *stands behind her and touches her as she speaks.*)

FLORIA: He put his hand not on my neck but on my breast. Don't touch me. I am not your food. I am not prey.

ACT ONE

(Scene shift)

(FLORIA *and* WEYLAND *in session*)

FLORIA: What actually happened at Cayslin?

WEYLAND: I hunted a woman. She was armed—a rapist had been active on the campus. She must have thought I was him. She shot me. I had to withdraw to heal.

FLORIA: You ran away.

WEYLAND: As best I could, yes.

FLORIA: Was she hurt?

WEYLAND: I was the one who was hurt. She nearly killed me.

FLORIA: Why hasn't she told them about you at Cayslin?

WEYLAND: Perhaps she thought no one would believe her. She was a foreigner of low status, on the housekeeping staff. I hear that she has returned home.

FLORIA: I suppose it takes silver bullets to kill a vampire.

WEYLAND: I was wearing a thick coat at the time, and the gun was small and cheap. And I haven't lived this long without luck.

FLORIA: Were you afraid?

WEYLAND: I was in shock, in pain, bleeding, I thought I was dying—yes, I was afraid.

FLORIA: And this woman, what about her? Can you speak for her fear?

WEYLAND: Why should I? It's nothing to me. You speak for her, Doctor. Better still, speak for yourself. I know why I'm a vampire. Why are you a therapist? To get your little sup of truth from each of your clients? Such paltry stuff, such fretful little lives. No wonder a great, monstrous truth intoxicates you. I feel you thinking after me sometimes, trying to look over my shoulder, prodding at my mind: how do you feel, what does this mean, speak for your anger, your anxiety, your boredom. You track me. You hunt me. You want me.

(Scene shift)

(FLORIA, *alone, working*)

KENNY: *(Offstage)* I don't care. I want to see her now. *(He bursts into the office.)* I know why you're trying to unload me. It's that new guy, the one with the profile, right? What is he, an old actor? Anybody can see you've got the hots for him.

FLORIA: Kenny, you have to pay for the privilege of verbal abuse and this isn't your hour.

KENNY: Listen, that guy isn't interested in you, Doctor, because he's a fruit. A faggot.

FLORIA: What he is or isn't is none of your business, Kenny.

KENNY: Yeah? Well, I've been following him. Yesterday he walked around like he does, and then he went into a movie house on Third that shows weird foreign movies—you know, Japs cutting each other's things off and like that—

FLORIA: Kenny, for Christ's sake—

KENNY: Well, there was a guy came in, a Brooks Brothers type carrying a briefcase. Your man moved over to sit behind him, and after a while he started sort of stroking Brooks Brothers' neck. The guy leaned back and your man leaned forward, like, nuzzling him, you know—kissing him. I saw it.

FLORIA: Now just stop right there—

KENNY: I mean it was disgusting, complete strangers, without even Hello. Brooks Brothers sat there with his

ACT ONE

head back, like zonked, you know, just swept away. He stayed like that after your fruity friend left. When the movie was over I waited outside, and out comes Brooks Brothers looking all sleepy and loose, like after you know what.

FLORIA: Kenny, you're fired.

KENNY: Fired? What do you mean, fired?

FLORIA: I will not have a client who spies on my other clients.

KENNY: You can't just kick me out!

FLORIA: We've already discussed finding a different therapist for you.

KENNY: I don't want a different therapist!

FLORIA: I'm sorry, Kenny. There are some things you simply are not allowed to do.

KENNY: I hate you. *(He runs out of the office.)*

FLORIA: *(To the intercom)* Hilda? Close the file on Kenny—no more appointments. *(She switches off the intercom.)* My God. What have I gotten myself into? Weyland, what are you?

(Curtain)

END OF ACT ONE

ACT TWO

(Scene: FLORIA *and* LUCILLE, *lunch break)*

LUCILLE: Kenny told you this? The Kenny we all know and love, right? And you're saying this story proves that your client really is a vampire?

FLORIA: Kenny didn't know what he was seeing. I do. It was exactly the way the client describes his hunting.

LUCILLE: I knew there was a problem when you stopped giving Hilda your tapes to transcribe. I'll get somebody else for the colloquium, and it's nothing to do with Jacoby or anybody else, just you. I prescribe a full-scale retreat, my girl.

FLORIA: I can't. Not now.

LUCILLE: I'll ask Hilda to start arranging temporary referrals for your clients.

FLORIA: I can't refer this one to anybody, Lucille. He's dangerous.

LUCILLE: Then he doesn't belong in your office, he belongs in a psychiatric hospital. You do too, if you're buying into his fantasy. You're a shrink, he's a nut, try to keep that straight, okay? And if you can't, then get him to somebody else pronto.

FLORIA: Lucille, just humor me, help me think my way through this. Suppose my vampire is for real, not a mythical revenant but an honest-to-God predatory animal that looks like a man—

LUCILLE: Okay, that's enough. I don't listen to nut-talk unless I'm getting paid.

FLORIA: You can't just dismiss it like that. His story hangs together at every point. I challenge, I push, but nothing gives, there are no gaps.

LUCILLE: He's just another clever psychotic who makes lying into an art-form.

FLORIA: He is a brilliant liar, that's how he survives; but he doesn't lie to me. I know by now when a client is lying. It's the process, Luce—he can't resist it. Think how seductive it must be to tell your deepest secrets to someone trained to listen—to speak safely in your real voice for the first time ever in a totally false life. It all makes sense because it's true.

LUCILLE: This is your idea of sense? Floria, don't try to rope me into this professional irresponsibility with you. You're dipping into your client's sickness instead of treating it. That's not therapy, it's collusion.

FLORIA: There is no sickness to dip into. As a human being of course he's off the charts, but as a vampire he's perfectly healthy. My god, did I just say that?

LUCILLE: This is a joke, right? You're pulling my leg.

FLORIA: No, Luce. I mean it. I think he's real.

LUCILLE: Well, you'd better get some harder evidence than a story from Kenny if you're going to talk to me about this, kiddo. But remember, if you insist on proof you just might push him into acting out his fantasies. Someone could get hurt, and frankly I wouldn't blame the client. I'd blame you.

(Scene shift)

(FLORIA *and* WEYLAND *in session*)

WEYLAND: You have no questions today, Doctor?

ACT TWO

FLORIA: I do have a question. No, a request—a demand, a condition. Promise me that no one from this office, no one connected with me, will be your prey.

WEYLAND: Ah. You're afraid.

FLORIA: If we're to continue I need your promise, do you understand?

WEYLAND: Better than you do, Doctor. What will you make of me with this therapy of yours? A predator paralyzed by empathy with his prey? A hunter fit only for a cage and a keeper? Your process is effective, and you use it well: I begin to see myself. But do you see yourself? The woman in a field of flowers with the unicorn, how gently she cajoles him: "Unicorn, come lay your head in my lap. You are a wonder, and for love of wonder I will tame you. Leash your pride and power, gaze at yourself in my mirror, rest under my hand—while the hunters close in to destroy you."

FLORIA: Promise.

WEYLAND: Well, then; I won't hunt here.

FLORIA: Why hunt at all? There are blood banks. Some people would feed you just for the thrill of it; Hell, they'd pay for the privilege.

WEYLAND: Technology, marketing—all that's just a phase. I have to keep my hunting skills sharp for your next Dark Age.

FLORIA: Then how about a night club act: silk-lined cape, spacy music, stage fog. Make the right substances available and no one would care what you drank.

WEYLAND: Don't try to trivialize what I am.

FLORIA: I don't have to trivialize what you are. Everyday reality trivializes what you are.

WEYLAND: I think I hear the gallumphing tread of the evening news. What is it this time? Poison gas in a hospital? A bomb in a school-bus?

FLORIA: A death squad officer displaying a corpse exhumed from a mass grave—part of a corpse, a V of stiff legs, empty groin, no feet. He held it up by one ankle, like a dead tree. He was smoking a cigar.

WEYLAND: Against the stink, no doubt. Why watch? I prefer basketball, a quick, graceful game, no corpses, no cigars. Don't look at me like that. I have no part in the outrages men commit against one another. My hunting is benign by comparison, modest and economical. Trivial, even.

FLORIA: That dead thing was someone's brother, someone's father, someone's child. For that matter, so is the man in uniform who knows just where to dig. Isn't he a predator, of sorts?

WEYLAND: Perhaps, but not of my sort. Why so angry, Doctor? We're just talking politics here, like one human being to another; the conversation of your kind.

FLORIA: My kind! You don't know anything about my kind.

WEYLAND: I know your secrets, the ones that go with being someone's sister, someone's father, someone's child: that you loved your parents too much and they didn't love you enough, only later it turned out to have been the other way around, or else just as you thought but much better, or much worse. The things you held dearest you never spoke of, or your words were so clumsy that no one understood. In turn you mistook what others meant and now it's too late. Your culture is woven of these so-called secrets which each of you hugs to your breast in what you are convinced is your own unique, incomparable guilt.

ACT TWO

FLORIA: I see you've been reading my case files. But you can't understand any of it if you feel no guilt. And you don't, do you? You're proud of living the way you do.

WEYLAND: I'm not ashamed. How can there be guilt where there is so little choice? I live according to necessity, like any animal. Perhaps that's why, intellect aside, I have the inner life of the average housecat. You noticed this, surely? Sometimes I look at my own secrets as you draw them from me—plain sense, for the most part, the logistics of a hunter's life—and I am ashamed to be so simple. There should be complex perceptions to go with the age and the magnitude of what I am. There should be wisdom to set me unmistakably apart from the torturer with the cigar. I have to be clever to survive and to keep myself entertained. But am I wise?

(FLORIA *does not reply.*)

WEYLAND: Perhaps my question is beyond our scope here. You look tired today.

FLORIA: I am tired.

WEYLAND: Then rest.

(*Scene shift*)

(FLORIA *dreams:* WEYLAND *enters and attacks her.*)

FLORIA: *(Fighting him off)* Get away from me! What are you doing?

WEYLAND: What you want me to do.

FLORIA: You bastard! Is that the famous imperceptible attack, the suave seducer's pounce that leaves no trace? Jesus, what a liar you are! Do you fuck them while you drink and pretend that's what they want?

WEYLAND: You do want it, all of you—sex and death together. All I want is my dinner.

FLORIA: Well damn it, you're not getting it here. I am not your victim.

WEYLAND: No, you're not. Others are, but not you. Why is that, Doctor Landauer?

FLORIA: Oh, fuck you. I'm not in the mood to play therapist.

WEYLAND: I thought the one you fuck is your lover.

FLORIA: When you talk about love, that's when I know I'm dreaming.

(WEYLAND *withdraws.*)

FLORIA: Only dreaming, of what I long for, what I fear, the way people do. Just a dream.

(Scene shift)

(FLORIA *and* LUCILLE)

FLORIA: What's this message that you left on my desk this morning?

LUCILLE: It's from your daughter. Remember your daughter Sarah? She calls me because she can't get through to you. You have no time for her, you have no time for anybody including the colleague you share an office with. Only for your vampire.

FLORIA: *(Reading message)* "What's wrong, Mom? Lucille wrote me the weirdest note, very cryptic and ominous." What the hell did you tell her?

LUCILLE: Something weird, cryptic, and ominous, I guess. Be grateful. It has crossed my mind to write something plain, detailed, and damning to the Oversight Committee of the State Board.

FLORIA: Lucille, this is my case. Stay out of it.

LUCILLE: Fine. One other thing: I don't suppose you've noticed, but Hilda's pretty upset. Kenny's aunt keeps calling the office, crying. Hilda says she told you.

ACT TWO   35

FLORIA: For Pete's sake, Luce, what am I supposed to do? Kenny is no longer my client. That was the idea, remember?

LUCILLE: His aunt wants to know who's keeping an eye on him now that he's refused to see another therapist. He doesn't answer his phone, his aunt is worried sick. Floria, have you noticed that your life is getting completely away from you lately? Have you considered therapy for yourself?

FLORIA: Jesus Christ.

(Scene shift)

(FLORIA and WEYLAND in session)

WEYLAND: *(Leafing through a book)* You call me Weyland now, not Edward.

FLORIA: A first name signifies intimacy. Your parents name you, your sisters and brothers call you by that name, your childhood friends use it. But you're not a man, you never were a child. Where did you get your name?

WEYLAND: I took it from a tombstone.

FLORIA: Be the book in your hands. What does it say?

WEYLAND: "I am old and full of knowledge. I am well made, I last longer than my reader. My pages are not for your eyes. Only my title shows." This is a good game.

FLORIA: The book's title is *Memory*. Open it and read to me.

WEYLAND: "I prefer to stay closed." That's what the book says.

FLORIA: Weyland, speak for memory.

WEYLAND: No. I never look backward. You have no idea of the risks involved.

FLORIA: Don't you know yet that you come here to take risks? The past can be a great teacher. What's so threatening about memory?

WEYLAND: Its depth. Your memory is one thin sheet of paper, mine is a whole volume of pages. I might lose my place.

FLORIA: Listen to me: in this office nothing can harm you. I make it safe for you to explore. Lend memory your voice. I haven't let you down yet, have I?

WEYLAND: No.

FLORIA: I haven't, and I won't. Let memory speak.

WEYLAND: Memory says, "I am heavy with time. I accumulate. I am as real as the life around you, but distilled to a greater strength. I offer beauty as well as pain. Let me in."

FLORIA: Take what memory has to give you. Open your mind. Try.

WEYLAND: Night. Horses. Smoke from the camp as I move past. The ground here outside the perimeter is churned and slippery. Voices—shouts, murmurs. I am hungry. Between me and the battlefield stands a sentry, white cross-belts gleaming in the dark. Beyond him wounded men lie bleeding, unnoticed among the dead. But I know they are there, I take their scent from the reeking wind. I barely feel the cold, but I am hungry.

FLORIA: Answer. Weyland, take back your voice and answer.

WEYLAND: Leave me, let me go! *(To* FLORIA*)* You see? The past is strong, and it never dies. Do you think you'll always be here to say, "Take back your voice, open your eyes?" You won't. You'll be gone, and I'll still be here.

ACT TWO

(Scene shift)

FLORIA: *(To recorder)* What am I to do with these secrets of his? Nobody has been in this territory, nobody. Nothing works the way it's supposed to. I lurch from terror to exhilaration and back again. Horses, crossbelts—what battlefield, how long ago? A huge, rich cloak of time flows back from his shoulders like the wings of a dark angel, but he can't look back, there are too many dangers ahead. I'm one of those dangers now, me and my big mouth full of artful questions. "You'll be gone," he said. Dead, he meant. You'll be dead. He himself could make that happen tomorrow; tonight. People die all the time over smaller secrets than the ones I've heard from him. I should tell Douglas that his prize professor is crazy as a loon, and let Weyland fend for himself, whatever he is. I still don't know, not for certain. Maybe Lucille is right, maybe I'm the crazy one.

(Scene shift)

(FLORIA *and* WEYLAND *in session*)

FLORIA: Weyland, can you show yourself to me in your true form?

WEYLAND: What are you asking, exactly?

FLORIA: Give me proof that you are what you say you are.

WEYLAND: Proof? You're not proposing to become my prey?

FLORIA: God, no. But there must be some physical, observable evidence—

WEYLAND: I've told you, my survival depends on being able to pass as a man.

FLORIA: If you're exactly like a man in every detail then you are a man, and I am a prize idiot.

WEYLAND: You know the truth. You've known it for weeks.

FLORIA: That's not enough. Give me proof.

WEYLAND: Proof will change things. Are you very sure you want it?

FLORIA: I'm very sure.

WEYLAND: There is something you can see.

(Scene shift)

FLORIA: *(Alone, to recorder)* He has no fangs, of course, or he could never smile—and human beings do smile, even the coldest of us. There's a sort of sting under his tongue. Simple, he says. Unobtrusive, painless. It's impossible, but I saw it. Which puts us—where? He must have planned to give up his "delusion", thank me for curing him, and return to work. God. He tried to do it and I wouldn't let him. It's impossible now. Something else will have to happen, but what? All his behavior springs from the stark, primary truth of being a predator who lives on human blood, a killer when necessary. Yet clarity, simplicity, and magnificence also rise from that basic animal integrity. Of course I long for that, here in the hodge-podge of my messy human life. But mess is human. How we deal with that mess expresses our integrity. Or how we refuse to deal with it. *(She makes a phone call.)* Sarah? I want to—look, do you think you could arrange to leave the kids with Keith, just for a little, and meet me at the cabin for some vacation time together? We really need to talk, Sare. What? Lucille shouldn't have involved you—wait. I didn't say that right. Lucille is upset over a professional problem of mine that I can't discuss with you. That's not what's all crossed up between you and me. Other things are, and I'd like us to take a crack at them. I called to invite—to ask you to go to the country with me so we can hang out a while, just the two of

ACT TWO

us. No, I'm not telling you what you need—it's what I need, Sarah. Don't answer yet, just think about it, all right? Take some time to think about it.

(Scene shift)

(FLORIA *and* WEYLAND *in session*)

WEYLAND: Who sent flowers? Dean Sharpe?

FLORIA: My daughter sent them. A peace offering, I hope.

WEYLAND: You have a child? How odd. I think of you as unique.

FLORIA: I am. Children aren't duplicates of their parents.

WEYLAND: So people keep trying for better copies, is that it?

FLORIA: You should be pleased to see your livestock increase and multiply.

WEYLAND: Pleased? I'm appalled. I continually reinvent myself, consuming only my modest share, while the world reels under the weight of your madly multiplying progeny.

FLORIA: Progeny? There's a word that has nothing to do with real kids.

WEYLAND: What do you expect? Speech isn't natural to me, it's a human invention. As a singular being, to whom would I speak if not for the requirements of life in the human herd?

FLORIA: Why do you speak to me? Why do you still come here? You must know I won't send—what you are—back to Cayslin. Not now. Not ever.

WEYLAND: Other plans are in motion, Cayslin doesn't matter any more. You do, though. So fearful, yet so persistent and inventive. It's your daring that draws me here now. I told you proof would change things.

FLORIA: But it hasn't. Nothing's changed. You're the same as when you first walked in here, you might as well never have come.

WEYLAND: So greedy! I open the fortress of myself, I show you rooms and views that I myself have never seen, and it's not enough?

FLORIA: I want more than a strip tease. Show me insight, show me transformation.

WEYLAND: There speaks your ambition, Doctor—not your best quality, I might add. You think that with a light pickling in your "process" I could be reborn, weak and confused like you, with one tiny life to live, like you. And I'm to cooperate in this miserable exchange. Well, I decline. I prefer the mastery of my own kind of life.

FLORIA: You have no life, only dreams of living, a little shadow-play between oblivions.

WEYLAND: Sour grapes, Doctor Landauer. You die, I sleep. You rot, I wake.

FLORIA: You hope. Well, you don't really know, do you? You don't remember.

WEYLAND: I know what I need to know. Do you think I arrived in the present as you see me? I woke as fragile as a starved bird, naked, dark, and shriveled, with an empty mind except for hunger. Edward Weyland is something that I made, through struggle, cunning, and talent, of course. Imagine coping all unprepared with your frantic times. Could you do that? I did. That's why you admire me just as I am. I'm not the one you are so desperate to change.

(Scene shift)

ACT TWO 41

(KENNY *and* LUCILLE *enter and comment from other parts of the stage.*)

KENNY: You think he's really something, don't you?

WEYLAND: That little man is still following me, the one I used to see here at your office.

FLORIA: Kenny! He's harmless. He's just trying to get at me.

LUCILLE: Okay, let's say he is what you say he is. So why haven't you called the cops? What is it, you and him against the world? The outlaw's gal is faithful to the end?

WEYLAND: He complicates my hunting.

LUCILLE: Let me tell you about Billy the Kid's girl. She's a coward. She gets to watch old Billy act out all her rage and frustration for her, but she never gets her own hands bloody. Your outlaw comes home and tells you what he did today at the office; maybe he tells you in bed; and it's a thrill for you, isn't it?

KENNY: I can't make out what he's after, exactly.

LUCILLE: To other people your vampire does something he thinks of as drinking their blood. Maybe he's not so nice with them, you know?

FLORIA: You let Kenny alone!

WEYLAND: Why? What makes him sacred?

LUCILLE: Floria, you have responsibilities here.

FLORIA: You touch Kenny and the authorities will make the connection with me, with you. Hell, I'll make the connection for them.

WEYLAND: Go ahead. Let them look for Professor Weyland; he'll be gone. I made this identity, I've already begun to make another—a shy, quiet drifter in denim and work boots doing odd jobs in diners and gas stations. No one sees such people.

KENNY: Sometimes he sort of melts into a crowd and I lose him. It's creepy.

FLORIA: You'll never do it. You're spoiled, you love the comforts of your Weyland-life.

WEYLAND: Yes. A rougher road would be good for me. It would remind me of my strengths.

KENNY: What's so great about him anyway? So he's old, he's had time to go places, maybe meet some famous people, pick up flashier kinks than most guys have. So what? He still has to put his pants on one leg at a time, just like everybody else.

WEYLAND: Even if you cleared me to return to Cayslin, I couldn't go back. No one is there for Professor Weyland to talk to as Edward Weyland talks to you, no one to listen as you listen—closely, without preconceptions or facile judgments. You are yourself one of the comforts of my Weyland-life—and a perilous one for me. No one knows me as you do and no one should. I must be someone who is content not to be known.

LUCILLE: I know you, Floria. At school you dazzled us all. I was in Heaven when you asked me to practice with you. Nobody knows you as well as I do. I can't believe you're throwing everything away.

FLORIA: Remember what it's like when you're a girl and your mind wanders while you're doing homework or washing dishes? You see yourself in a field of flowers attended by the unicorn. Only you are allowed to share the solitude of this unique and pristine monarch of the enchanted forest. The hounds and the hunters he gores to bloody rags, which is terrible and pitiable but wonderful too. Because to you and you alone all his danger and his beauty and his magic defer.

LUCILLE: I am not your mother. You have no right to break my heart.

(Scene shift)

KENNY: *(Speaking on pay phone)* Suppose a person doesn't happen to be old and suave. Nobody starts out like that. You try to copy the people who know, but everybody just laughs. It's like being a baby all your life in a world full of grown-ups, and nobody will help you get the hang of things. The people who should help you kick you out because they're sick of you, they think you're stupid. But it's just that everything is so scary that you can't concentrate. You do things wrong—too slow, too fast, too loud, whatever. That doesn't make you garbage, to be thrown away as soon as some slick old creep shows up who knows how to get around anybody, and I do mean anybody. You should see some of the people he spends time with. You wouldn't be so hot for him to jump your bones then. But why listen to me, I'm just dumb Kenny who doesn't know anything. Only I'm no dummy, and that guy's a creep. I'll prove it, you'll see.

(Scene shift)

*(*FLORIA *alone.* LUCILLE *enters.)*

FLORIA: Don't scold me, Luce. I'm not up for it today.

LUCILLE: We're way past that. Doug Sharpe has been trying to reach you for days and you don't call him back, and Hilda says you've rescheduled every client but one.

FLORIA: I wish Hilda would mind her own damn business.

LUCILLE: One of the people she works for is going off the deep end. That is her business, and mine too. You've let this guy seduce you.

FLORIA: For Christ's sake, Lucille, I am not sleeping with my client.

LUCILLE: So how come his appointments are regularly running overtime? What are you two doing in here, analyzing the bond market?

FLORIA: I know it looks terrible—

LUCILLE: No, not terrible. Outrageous. Inexcusable. Floria, it's the men who screw their clients and cover for each other. We have to be better than that. It's not fair, but we have to. You can't do this. You can't.

FLORIA: Luce, I am in trouble, okay? But—

LUCILLE: So what are you going to do about it?

FLORIA: What are you going to do? I saw the draft of your letter to the oversight people. Are you going to send it?

LUCILLE: If I have to. You're in breach of your professional ethics. You're a disgrace to every woman in practice and a danger to your clients. That's bad enough but, Floria, if you make me turn you in for it I will never, ever forgive you.

(Scene shift)

(WEYLAND, *alone in the office, night. The phone rings. Hearing* FLORIA *approach he conceals himself.* FLORIA *enters.*)

KENNY: *(Live on message machine)* Doctor Landauer? I'm still woozy from all the dope they gave me. I'm at Roosevelt Hospital. God, I'm so scared—he jumped me. He was cruising the hock shops and the thrift stores, buying old clothes, a backpack and stuff. He caught me watching him. He hurt me. I'm scared he might—hello? Oh, be there, please! Hello?

FLORIA: *(Picks up phone)* Kenny? Are you all right?

KENNY: Everything hurts. He broke my arm, my ribs. What if he goes after you too? I didn't mean to make trouble for you.

FLORIA: It's all right, Kenny. You rest now. I'll come by in the morning, I promise.

(WEYLAND *emerges from the shadows.*)

FLORIA: What are you doing here?

WEYLAND: I want all your notes on my case, Doctor Landauer. I've taken what I could find, including your colleague's rather unflattering letter to the authorities.

FLORIA: You have no right—

WEYLAND: Not right, necessity. Professor Weyland is no longer a viable identity for me, thanks to you. He must vanish again, this time for good. So must your notes on the man he was, a man who knew how to make himself disappear. These superficial jottings can't be all you've done.

FLORIA: I do have a practice, you know. There's only so much time for each client.

WEYLAND: How many are vampires? You meant to write a paper about me, maybe even a book. Give me your notes.

FLORIA: No. What are you going to do about it, beat me up the way you beat up Kenny? You promised me—

WEYLAND: I warned you. He was watching me assemble my new persona, piece by piece. He's identified me to the police, hasn't he? It doesn't matter—not without your records to support his story. Not without you.

FLORIA: Leave Kenny alone. He'll listen to me, he won't say anything—

WEYLAND: Promises, negotiations—I thought you would be brave. Give me what I've asked for.

FLORIA: *(Gives him notes)* What now?

WEYLAND: You know. It's been coming since you first believed me, and I saw your fear.

FLORIA: Christ. I will not be your goddamn prey.

WEYLAND: Don't belittle yourself, I've had my meal today. But the tenth floor is a long way from the sidewalk, and the suicide rate among therapists is notoriously high. I looked it up.

FLORIA: You can't do it.

WEYLAND: Think of it as an artistic ending, satisfying if not exactly neat. You were named for the heroine of an opera, weren't you? She kills herself, leaping from a castle wall. People are so careless in the names they give their children.

FLORIA: If I meant to expose you I'd have done it by now.

WEYLAND: You could swear to keep my secret, and mean it, and turn me in tomorrow on a simple human impulse.

FLORIA: Look at me, Weyland. My eyes are your mirror, my mind is your mirror.

WEYLAND: Mirrors can be broken.

FLORIA: Then who will see you, who will give you back to yourself as you really are?

WEYLAND: A vampire must have no reflection. Either the mirror breaks, or I do.

FLORIA: Let me touch you.

WEYLAND: No more therapy, Doctor, that's over.

ACT TWO 47

FLORIA: I want you to make love with me.

WEYLAND: You know I can't be bribed that way. What are you up to? Are you one of those who come into heat at the sight of an upraised fist?

FLORIA: No. It's you I want, not some fantasy of erotic agony. And I'm not saying "Love me now, kill me later." Understand me, Weyland: if death is your answer, I'll fight with everything I've got, I'll do you as much damage as I can. But if you can trust my silence and let me go, then this is how we ought to end our time together. This is the completion I want. You want it, too.

WEYLAND: Isn't it extremely unprofessional to proposition a client?

FLORIA: Extremely. I've never done it before, and I never will again. For you to indulge in a courtship that doesn't end in a meal is unprofessional too; but how would it feel, this once? Let me touch you.

WEYLAND: It's too dangerous to let you live. Why do I want to do this?

FLORIA: Because you don't have to. It won't promote your survival, it's not one of your your animal necessities. This is something you choose, for yourself.

WEYLAND: I know "making love" as part of the hunt. This is different, isn't it?

FLORIA: Yes, this is different. Put your hand on my face, like this. We touch each other, gently, that's how we begin. We talk softly and move close.

(Scene shift)

(FLORIA *and* WEYLAND, *night*)

FLORIA: What are you doing?

WEYLAND: Thinking. I think I should have killed you.

FLORIA: It was that good for you? I'm joking. People sometimes make jokes to cover hurt feelings. Weyland, talk to me.

WEYLAND: That little man, I should have killed him too. But he called your name like a dying man calling for his mother or praying to his god. So I let him live.

FLORIA: Be glad you did. If you had killed that boy—

WEYLAND: What? What would you have done? You can say the word, I already know it: betray. There are so many Kennys and only one of me. You'd think I would have at least some scarcity value.

FLORIA: My God, one half hour of warmth in your whole glacial existence and all you have to offer is complaints and accusations? Is this what a little tenderness does for you? Good thing you don't have a taste for it.

WEYLAND: You're being deliberately obtuse. If I can't bring myself to destroy people who threaten me, no matter who they are or who they love, I can't survive.

FLORIA: Yes you can—not as a monster, as a man. Is it so terrible to nourish another instead of only feeding on what you can take?

WEYLAND: Yes. It is against my nature.

FLORIA: You don't know what your nature is. Your life at Cayslin used only a fraction of your potential, and you were so bored that you smashed your way out. There are still so many secrets. You knew you could have sex with people, but you didn't know that you could make love. It's human not to know our limits. You're so close, and it's terrifying because the stakes are high. But imagine what you might teach and learn, what you might grow to be—

ACT TWO

WEYLAND: I don't want to grow. I want myself back as I was. But there is no more Weyland. You have consumed him.

FLORIA: Don't feel so sorry for yourself. For what it's worth, Floria the therapist is dead too. You're not the only one with rules, you know. Rule number one: don't sleep with your clients. I'm through here, my professional life is over.

WEYLAND: That is a pity. You're very good.

FLORIA: Well, I'll have to be very good at something else. Any ideas? You've reinvented yourself a hundred times, you know how it's done. Advise me. I can't just change my clothes and hitchhike into the sunset.

WEYLAND: And you think I can? What happens when I meet someone not even as trustworthy as you, but I trust them anyway because I'm starved for the sweet thrill of trust? It's impossible for me, this craving to be close. One great hunger is all I can afford.

FLORIA: Wait—you can't be Weyland any more, you can't start over—what are you going to do?

WEYLAND: Think, Doctor, what's left? I have my own way home—call it Plan C, nice and simple, for a simple animal. All I have to do is close my eyes and sleep.

FLORIA: No. No. That's the worst thing you could do! Awake you can react, think, defend yourself. Comatose in some dirty subway tunnel, what are you? A helpless lump at the mercy of the whole world, and there is no mercy.

WEYLAND: No, there isn't. I should drink you dry and walk away without a backward glance, whole again. But I don't want to feel what I would feel if you were dead. You see? I can't act to protect myself now, awake and aware. I'm at the world's mercy as it is.

FLORIA: So your solution is to turn tail and run, to hide in some hole in the ground and forget everything, until you wake up again one day as cold and empty as a cruising shark? That's what you want?

WEYLAND: Yes. Yes. I'm sorry to spoil your romantic vision of me, but courage is not one of my qualities. I wouldn't have lived this long if it were.

FLORIA: That's crap. You've been running on sheer nerve for weeks. I've watched you.

WEYLAND: That wasn't my courage, it was yours, you lent it to me. I need to give it back now.

FLORIA: You can't. You can't just turn your back on what we've achieved together and ask me to bless your cowardice.

WEYLAND: Floria, you are unjust. I don't deserve your contempt.

FLORIA: I'm not asking you to stay with me. I can settle for knowing you're still prowling around out there somewhere. But this—it's too hard, it's too much like death.

WEYLAND: Is it part of making love, to afterwards make pain?

FLORIA: You can't do this to me. I will not be cast as the temptress, the shallow, greedy woman whose touch destroys the magical beast.

WEYLAND: What are you complaining about? The destroyer is the one who survives.

FLORIA: Damn you, you came to me, not the other way around; and you stayed, you elected to stay. Oh, Weyland, why did you ever let me tamper with you?

WEYLAND: I thought your games were harmless because they drew no blood.

FLORIA: I never meant it to end this way.

ACT TWO

WEYLAND: You could do worse. To lose your career for an aging academic with a bizarre mid-life crisis—how banal, even comical. But to lose it for a monster of mythic proportions—there is grandeur in that.

FLORIA: For you. I never meant it to end like this for you. I wanted to liberate you.

WEYLAND: Then do it. Say goodbye, sleep safe, sweet dreams. Say, I will remember you.

FLORIA: Go on then, run. Hide in the dirt like a blind, breathing stone. Lucky bastard—you get to sleep your way to your future. I have to deal with mine now. And you get to forget your dreams afterward, along with everything else, because you have to. You're not built to carry so much loss. How many times have you run this same course before? I can't be the first ever to drag you to the brink of humanity, and then lose you. I could have kept you, though. I could have made chains of words, lies and persuasions strong enough to hold even you. Only we got into the habit of telling the truth, and I won't give that up. Everything else, but not that. So go on, go away, go deep in the earth where no one can find you. Close your eyes, let go, forget. I'm the one that's human. I'll remember for us both.

(Curtain)

END OF PLAY

www.ingramcontent.com/pod-product-compliance
Lightning Source LLC
Chambersburg PA
CBHW072017060426
42446CB00043B/2637